Speak Your Pet's Language!

Discover:

- How animals "see" our thoughts . . . even when we don't say them out loud
- How to communicate through colors, images, and feelings
- New ways of explaining things to your pet
- Tips for keeping new behaviors on track
- How to resolve human–pet issues
- How to thank your pet for listening and for his unconditional love

Whether you share your life with a diva dog, a finicky feline, a high-handed horse, or a precocious parrot, this remarkable guide will open the door to the intuitive understanding you need to get more deeply in touch with your pet, as you both discover how to experience the world in an amazing new way.

Judy Meyer has been changing the lives of pets and their people as a telepathic communicator since 1990. She has over eight hundred clients throughout the world, including Fox TV, the Houston Police Department, and several Kentucky Derby winners. She lives in Santa Fe.

THE ANIMAL CONNECTION

A Guide
to Intuitive

Communication with
Your Pet

Judy Meyer

A PLUME BOOK

PLUME
Published by the Penguin Group
Penguin Putnam Inc., 375 Hudson Street,
New York, New York 10014, U.S.A.
Penguin Books Ltd, 27 Wrights Lane, London W8 5TZ, England
Penguin Books Australia Ltd, Ringwood, Victoria, Australia
Penguin Books Canada Ltd, 10 Alcorn Avenue,
Toronto, Ontario, Canada M4V 3B2
Penguin Books (N.Z.) Ltd, 182–190 Wairau Road,
Auckland 10, New Zealand

Penguin Books Ltd, Registered Offices:
Harmondsworth, Middlesex, England

First published by Plume, a member of Penguin Putnam Inc.

First Printing, May, 2000
1 3 5 7 9 10 8 6 4 2

 REGISTERED TRADEMARK—MARCA REGISTRADA

LIBRARY OF CONGRESS CATALOGING-IN-PUBLICATION DATA:

Meyer, Judy.
The animal connection : a guide to intuitive communication with
your pet / Judy Meyer.
p.   cm.
ISBN 0-452-28174-1
1. Pets—Behavior. 2. Human–animal communication. 3. Animal
communication. I. Title.
SF412.5.M49 2000
636.088'7—dc21   99-049878

Printed in the United States of America
Set in Souvenir

FOR KISKA

A great master in my life
. . . the lessons never end

Acknowledgments

It seems impossible to thank everyone responsible for the life of this book, but here's who comes to mind . . .

I am grateful to Sandy for his forbearance, sacrifices, and monetary support. For their intricate personalities, wisdom, reflections, and lessons, I would like to thank my immediate family of animals: Kiska, Teal, Duke, Henry, Suki and Jupiter, Dinah, Bolo, Grace, and Topaz.

Much of what I have written in this book I learned from Penelope Smith, to whom I am grateful for kick-starting my memory. To Diane Fisher, I appreciate your helpful book mock-up.

To Jennie Dunham, I acknowledge your efforts in all areas as my literary agent. To my editors, Brian Tart and Jennifer Dickerson Kasius, I thank you for your patience and understanding.

A special, lifesaving award and thank you goes to Abby Remer for her organization, positive energy, and, most meaningfully, her love of animals, which produced an excellent proposal and final draft of manuscript. It was her persistence, as well as her time and attention, that made this book a reality.

The dedication and selflessness of the animals of this planet, wild and domestic, continually amazes me, and to them I am particularly grateful.

To my many clients here and abroad, I thank you for the opportunity of communicating with so many of these wondrous beings we call animals.

Preface

Obviously, if you have picked up this book you have a love of, a curiosity about, or at least some interest in animals, but for whatever reason you have chosen this book, *Welcome*.

First, let me say that we are all born with the ability to intuitively communicate with animals. Animals use this same intuitive method to communicate with one another, as well as with us, *if* we are willing to listen. And that's just what this little book is designed to do: To help you to speak to animals and remember your innate ability to communicate on an intuitive level so you can "hear" them as well. *The Animal Connection* contains the basic steps for this type of communication, which can be practiced at your own pace. Take the time to hear what your pet has to say. You'll both be greatly enriched.

A few things to keep in mind as you read this book:

- All living beings of this planet—whether human, animal, or plant—are created from the same energy; therefore, in the highest sense, no being is greater than any other.

- We don't "own" animals. They are not our possessions like some piece of furniture. Animals don't think of us as their owners, but as their people, just as we think of them as our bird, our dog, our cat, our horse, and so forth.

- The more intelligently you speak to an animal, the more intelligent the response will be.

- Cats, dogs, horses, birds, snakes, and all others are different species from us. Animals don't always understand *or care* about our rules for living just as we don't always understand theirs.

Finally, communicating with your pet can be tremendously rewarding, and I have found it to be the foundation for harmony that can help improve the quality of your life together.

Enjoy your journey!

Judy Meyer
March 1999

Introduction

When Bill called, he sounded a bit desperate. Pinkie, his darling, sweet, and lovable pit bull, was destroying his house whenever he left her there alone. I told Bill that in order to get her to stop this behavior we had to ask Pinkie what was causing it. When asked, Pinkie made it clear to me that she loved Bill so much that she just couldn't stand to have him out of her sight. Even though Bill worked at home and was really there a lot of the time for Pinkie, she had great difficulty whenever he was away from the house. I asked Bill to tell Pinkie why he sometimes had to leave her at home. He carefully explained to her that there were times when he had to take care of business and it was too hot for her to be left in the car. I also advised Bill that when he left, he needed to tell Pinkie where he was going, when he was coming back, what her job was to be while he was gone, and to end by thanking her. This type of direct communication is crucial. I assured him that she could understand what he was saying and deserved the same consideration he would give any person in this situation.

After Bill told all this to Pinkie, she communicated to me that she understood why Bill could not take her all the time, but she still insisted that she couldn't bear to be without him. Upon hearing this, Bill and I had to come up with some ideas to present to Pinkie in order to solve this problem. After some negotiation with the dog, we finally came up with a solution.

Pinkie agreed that if Bill were to leave one of his shirts with her, she would then leave the rest of the house alone. Before he left for town the next morning, Bill spoke to Pinkie. He told her he was going to run an errand and would be back at two o'clock that afternoon. He explained that her job was to keep the house in order, and he finished by thanking her. Bill then left Pinkie one of his shirts and went into town to take care of his errand. When he returned, Bill found his house in *perfect* order. And there, in the middle of his bed, sat Pinkie with his shirt and one lonely button, which she had carefully removed. That was good enough for him.

Does a simple story like this make you wonder what else animals have to say? What other reasons would you have to want to communicate in this manner with your pet? Maybe an animal that you had for a while was put up for adoption because he or she was peeing on your rugs and you just couldn't get your pet to stop. Possibly, you had a ferret that killed one of your birds, so you took him or her to an animal shelter, but to this day you still feel guilty about it, and you never want this to happen again. Or perhaps you had a pony that kept biting your children and it frightened you so much that you sold him, but your children cried when their beloved pony was gone. Maybe you had a cat that was ruining your furniture by scratching it, and you had his or her claws removed because you didn't have any idea how to get your cat to stop. Now you feel terrible about it because you know that removing a cat's claws is like removing the last joint of your fingers. Frequently, these types of problems, like others that arise when two different species are trying to coexist, can be solved by simple communication.

As an animal communicator, my job entails intuitively communicating with animals. Intuition is simply the ability to know or sense something without the use of traditional processes. It is immediate cognition, or what you might call perceptive insight.

In my day-to-day practice, clients and I speak with their animal companions about all sorts of issues, but most often they call because of some sort of behavioral problem. This problem could be anything from a dog getting out of a fenced yard, to a horse that is bucking off his rider, to a cat that just will not use the litter box, or a bird that continuously pulls out her feathers.

I begin the consultation by having the person talk directly to the animal. I then tell them to ask the animal one question at a time. I instruct them to ask a question because usually the person wants to know something. And that "something," many times, is *why* the animal is behaving in a certain way that the person feels is unacceptable. After the client asks the questions, there is a period of silence while I'm listening to the animal. I perceive words or pictures, but it's also possible to perceive feelings or colors. As soon as the animal has finished relating the information, I tell the person what has been communicated, and this progresses as a translated conversation. I am just a translator. I'm not a magician or a psychic.

This type of communication continues until we discover the root of the problem. Then, as in the case with Pinkie, we derive a solution that, hopefully, will work for everyone involved.

As a professional animal communicator, I have helped hundreds of clients with their animals' behavioral problems. I spend much of our sessions teaching them how to communicate with their animal companions. Once clients and their pets learn to communicate, they can better understand the role each plays in the other's life, as well as the significance of what I call "unacceptable" behavior. Just as I teach my clients how to communicate, this book will help you to communicate with the animals in your life and will bring both of you to a new level of understanding, respect, and love.

The ultimate purpose of my work, including this book, is to restore peace and harmony to people and their animal companions through communication. It's my contribution to improving life for the animals of this planet.

The secret to communicating with your animal can be summed up in just two steps . . .

(1) Talk to them.

(2) Listen to them.

It's not complicated.
It's really that simple.

Welcome to the journey.

PART I

Speaking to Your Animals

What to Say
and
How to Say It

Where do you begin?

Speak to your pet in an intelligent manner.

Pretend that it's Halloween. Someone in a cat suit appears at your door. Do you think that because that someone is disguised as a cat, he or she can't understand you? Of course not.

And this is what I tell my clients. I say, "Imagine that your animal is an intelligent being disguised as a cat, disguised as a dog, disguised as a bird, or a horse, or whatever fabulous species that has come to be with you, and speak to them in an intelligent manner."

It's important to dispel misconceptions about animals' intelligence before you attempt to communicate with your pet.

I'm sure you've heard some of these misconceptions, and many more, about the inferior intelligence of animals:

"Oh, they're just dumb animals."

"German shepherds are so smart they can understand fifty words."

"Cats have the intelligence level of a three-year-old, and horses only have the intelligence of a two-year-old."

It's vital to get past these false notions if you want to communicate on an intelligent level with your pet.

Here's how Richard realized the true intelligence of his animals. Richard explained that he worked quite a bit in his yard and loved having his two dogs with him, but whenever he let them out, they dashed across the street. Richard had no fence to keep them in the yard, and thinking there was no other solution, he kept the dogs locked in the house while he worked outside.

I informed Richard that animals really are quite intelligent, and if he would just speak to his dogs, they would stay in the yard. He regarded me with some skepticism, but I continued anyway, telling him how to set the boundaries for his dogs. I directed him to walk around the entire perimeter of his yard with the dogs on their leashes and, every third step or so, to tell them that this is the boundary in which he wanted them to stay.

Finally, I told Richard that before he let the dogs outside next time, he should say something like, "Okay, guys, you may come outside as long as you stay within the boundaries. Thank you."

A week later, Richard reported that he had spoken with his dogs. He seemed surprised, but thrilled, that they no longer run away. Now Richard enjoys their company as he works in the yard, reaping the benefits of trusting his dogs to understand what he was saying. Richard admits that now he talks to them about everything.

I have designed nine exercises sprinkled throughout the book to help you in communicating with your pet.

Exercise 1

Through the Eyes
of Your Animal

Another important step that will help you to communicate with your animal is to imagine the world from their point of view—from inside their body.

Pick any animal with whom you feel a certain connection.

- Close your eyes and imagine what it feels like to be in the body of that animal. Sense what it feels like to have four feet, or two feet if you are a bird, or eight legs if you choose a spider, and so on.

- Now feel the bottom of your feet touching the earth as you walk.

- Sense what it's like to be constantly on alert for predators.

- Feel the sun warming your fur as you curl up on the south side of the house, or the wind ruffling your feathers, or a falling twig jiggling your web.

- Keep visualizing, expanding on whatever helps you get in touch with a given animal.

This prepares you for the second exercise, which helps you realize an animal's intelligence.

Exercise 2

Recognizing an Animal's Intelligence

- Go back and think about something an animal did that made you think, "Wow, how did he know how to do that?" Or maybe you saw a newspaper article or a television program on an amazing rescue by an animal, like the gorilla who gently helped a child that had fallen into her cage, and you thought, "Now that's a really smart animal." Perhaps on the news you heard of a parrot that woke an older woman when a fire broke out and the whole household was saved.

- I have given you a few examples; now continue to recall as many instances as you can, noting the intelligence of these animals. It's up to you to recall your own experiences.

So, remember your own animal's intelligence when you begin to communicate.

*Speak to an animal in
the same manner you
would a person.*

For example, if you went with a friend to an outdoor café, you would never just walk away without saying something such as, "Wait here. Have a seat. I'll go get us some coffee and be right back."

The same idea applies when explaining things to your pet.

After one consultation, Kathleen quickly caught on to the concept of speaking to her dogs as she would a person. She took her dogs to a coffeehouse with an outdoor patio. Kathleen told her dogs to please lie down next to the table, to be quiet, and wait for her while she went inside to get them and herself a treat. She said they did exactly what she had asked, and they all had a lovely time. Kathleen could not believe how simple this was—that just speaking to her dogs as she would a friend could achieve such excellent results.

Speaking to your pet is such a simple thing.

Just say the words and your animal companion will get the message.

Why?

Because animals understand every word you say.

How do they understand your words? How can this be?

Because unbeknownst to you, whenever you utter a word, a mental image of that word flashes in your brain.

And, this is what your pet is able to see.

When you say, or even think, "I'm going to the car," a picture of you walking to your car flashes through your mind. You're not aware of this picture because it's so second nature to you, but your animal is thoroughly aware of it.

This is how they communicate with one another, and with us.

How many stories have you heard people tell of their dogs showing up at their car just as they were getting ready to leave and yet, a moment before, the dog was nowhere in sight?

Or what about stories people relate of not being able to find their cats, but suddenly the cat appears when the person is ready to feed them dinner?

This occurs because our animals see those pictures in our minds.

Exercise 3

Recognizing Silent Communication Between Animals

- Try to remember an instance when you've seen two animals communicate with each other.

For example, two dogs are resting side by side, and for no apparent reason they look at each other, and then in the next instant, they suddenly take off running. You didn't hear anything. There were no barks.

What do you think happened? They were, of course, communicating with each other using mental images.

- Now continue to think of times when you saw silent communication between two animals, whether domestic or in the wild.

Recognize that in all these instances, the animals were communicating by sending mental pictures to each other. You just hadn't yet learned how to notice.

If you want to see some concrete results when asking your animal to do something, be sure it's something they really want to do.

Especially when you first begin communicating in this new way, it's important to ask your animal companion to do something that you know she or he really enjoys: coming in to eat, playing with a ball, going for a ride in the car, or chasing a toy mouse on a string.

Here's a good example. My cat Henry refuses to use the cat door. I understand and respect his reasons for not using it, but this means I have to be his doorman. If he is outside on a cold night and I'm getting ready to go to bed, I'll call out the door, "Henry, I'm going to bed now, if you want to come in for the night, you'd better come now." In two minutes or less, I see a black streak that is Henry racing up to the door.

He comes because this is something he really wants to do.

If I had said, "Henry, come on. We're going to the vet now," I don't think I would see much of Henry for the next few hours.

An animal may misinterpret your thoughts when you say things in the negative.

You may be afraid that your dog is going to chase a car. In your mind, because of your fear, you actually visualize him chasing the car. You think to yourself, "Oh, no, Chumly's going to chase that car."

Out of your mouth come the words, "Chumly, don't chase the car." So what does Chumly do? He may perceive the mental picture, but not the words, and off he goes after the car.

Then you may think, "Oh, this communication stuff doesn't work," or some people may even think that Chumly is a stupid dog, but that's not the case at all.

Use Positive Redirection.

What you want to say is, "Chumly, please stay on the side of the road because cars can be dangerous and not everyone loves dogs the way I do. A car can hit you, can hurt you, and I would be so sad if something bad happened to you because I love you. That's why I'm asking you to stay on the side of the road. Thank you."

State your request to an animal in a positive way.

Say what you *do* want, not what you *don't* want.

I have found that stating a request in this manner goes a long way toward getting the appropriate results. "Kitty, I would like you to scratch your claws here on the sisal scratching post or on this nice log with bark," instead of, "Don't scratch the couch!"

Those of you who have children may already be aware of this method of positive redirection.

If I had just kept yelling "No!" at my cat Topaz when she would climb up on top of our kitchen cabinets and break my ceramic pots, I probably wouldn't have been able to get her to stop.

Rather, I explained to her that I made those pots, it makes me sad to see them broken, and it takes a lot of time for me to clean up the mess. I finished by saying, "Please be careful with my pots. Thank you."

Remember: She was seeing the pictures of my words as I spoke them. I didn't have to try hard to show her the pictures because I really meant what I was saying. When you do that, the pictures are just naturally there.

Topaz never broke another pot, even though she still gets up on top of the cabinets.

Exercise 4

Stating Things
in a Positive Way

- Before an incident occurs, it's a good idea to practice stating things in a positive way. Say something to your pet such as, "Zoë, please stay on your mat on the floor." Not, "Zoë, don't get on the sofa!"

- Or if you have a dog that jumps on people when they come to the door, you could say, "Sam, please keep all four feet on the floor when people come to the door." Avoid, "Sam, don't jump on people!"

- Practice this *before* the next person comes to the door. It helps establish a new way of speaking so that you correctly say what's needed as a situation arises.

- Continue saying out loud as many positive statements as you can think of that apply personally to you and your pet that may be necessary in any day-to-day situation.

Explain to your animals the reason you are asking them to do something.

Remember, animals are *intelligent,* and like people, they are more likely to respond better if you fully explain the reason behind your request.

That's why we tell Chumly that cars are dangerous, that he might get injured or killed, that we want him to be safe because we love him, and that is *why* we have requested that he stay on the sidewalk.

Nobody wants to be told, "Do it because I said so," including our animal companions, but that's what we imply if we just give our animals a command without an explanation.

And remember the love you have for your animal that, in the heat of the moment, you might lose sight of when trying to correct a behavior that you find aggravating or dangerous.

If animals can understand your thoughts, why don't they always do what you're thinking?

Animals *can* hear your thoughts because they *see* the pictures in your mind whether they are spoken out loud or thought silently.

There are several reasons why you might not see a response to your thoughts. One is that your pet may not necessarily be tuned in to your thoughts every moment of the day.

For example, you may have the television on all the time, but you may not necessarily hear every word until something catches your attention.

We think about all sorts of things that just don't interest our animals, like the mail, what we are going to wear, or some other thought that simply does not concern them.

Getting them to listen.

To get your animal's attention, first say his or her name. Then say or think what you want to tell your pet.

Sometimes your pets may actually be busy and may not be ready, or able, to listen to you at the moment, so it's important to get their attention.

Your animal companions are busy when they are eating, playing, going to the bathroom, or doing their job (such as barking at an intruder). Even when they look like they're doing nothing, they could be deep in thought. Remember, you wouldn't interrupt your friend if they were in the middle of a task. Use that same respect when speaking to your pet.

Sometimes you may need to give your pet a polite tap to get their attention.

I do this with my cats when I want to tell them something and they're not really busy but don't seem to be listening.

I give them a light tap on their head and then say, "Excuse me, I'm trying to tell you something. Could you please listen?"

Then I tell them what I want to say.

Animals can understand our words either way—spoken out loud or as silent thoughts.

As we saw, animals see our thoughts, even if we don't state them aloud.

I personally like to express my words out loud to them instead of as silent thoughts because it's more natural for me. I find that it helps me focus on exactly what I want to say.

But if you are very clear with the silent thoughts in your head, you can try communicating that way.

Whichever method you choose, you first have to get your animal's attention.

This is especially important if you have an animal that has difficulty hearing, whether it's due to deafness or to being hyperactive. (A hyperactive animal can more easily hear you after strenuous exercise—it's perfect for releasing excess energy, which can cause an animal to be distracted from what you are saying.)

Once you have gotten your animal's attention, he or she does not have to be looking at you to be listening.

You can tell when a person is listening, even if she or he isn't looking at you.

You just sense that they are paying attention or not.

The same is true with your animal.

*An animal's natural
state when you are
speaking to them is
one of three things . . .*

When I'm doing an animal-communication consultation, I find that most animals, once we get their attention, do one of three things.

They may:

- Look around at their environment
- Look like they are sleeping
- Stare at you

This last one is especially true when *you* ultimately have understood what an animal is trying to tell you. He or she may turn and stare right into your eyes. "Thank goodness," your pet says, "you finally got it!"

If an animal you are speaking to runs out of the room, or heads for the barn, or hops into the closet in the middle of the conversation . . .

. . . you can bet this means he doesn't want to talk about that particular subject!

Especially if the subject has to do with behavior *you* may consider unacceptable.

What do you do if an animal is being especially resistant to some important message you are trying to tell them?

First of all, avoid baby talk. It only defeats the idea that you're trying to get an important message across to your pet.

I would suggest that you hold your pet's face so that you can make eye contact with him or her while you are speaking. This lets an animal know you mean business and there is no room for movement in this particular situation.

When I say there is no room for movement, I mean this applies only to a critical situation, such as a cat blindly running into the street or a dog chasing the neighbor's cat, a horse continually bucking, or some other potentially dangerous situation.

There is no reason to rule with an iron hand unless the situation *is* serious.

My dog Kiska was a perfect example of a re-sistant animal. I found it almost impossible to hold his face. After all, he is a 120-pound mal-amute with a mind of his own, and he would jerk his head away if ever I would try to hold it. So, I used my wits and came up with another solution.

I had been trying to get him to stop running off with Buster, a neighborhood dog. Every time I attempted to talk to Kiska about the way he and Buster were terrorizing the other neighbor-hood dogs, he would simply walk away. He just would *not* listen to me and I could hear him say, "This is not a people thing" (meaning, this was between dogs and had nothing to do with me).

One day I had an idea.

I know how much Kiska likes sweets, so I bribed him. I told him if he would just listen, I would give him a cinnamon bun. He listened. I gave him the treat and was able to get through to him. He never ran off with Buster again.

I'm not advocating bribery, but be lovingly creative in getting your animal companion to listen to you if normal methods fail.

Respect your animal's free will.

We all have free will, including our pets. It's important to realize that just as *you* don't do everything you are told, neither will your animal companions.

You have your reasons for not doing something, and so do they.

When I say respect your animal's free will, I'm referring to fully grown, adult animals. Young animals, certainly under the age of one year, are essentially equivalent to human babies and young children. You can't expect them to comply with your verbal requests until they are at the age when they can reason and have developed some self-control. And just as with babies and young children, you may have to use physical restraint instead of trying to change their behavior, at least until they are older. For instance, if you don't want a kitten to continually climb on the table while you're eating, I would suggest containing them in another room until she or he is old enough to understand your words.

Take into consideration your animal's natural instincts if his or her behavior is not acceptable to you.

I have three dogs. Kiska is an Alaskan mala-mute; Duke, a golden retriever–cocker spaniel mix; and Dinah, a wolf–golden retriever mix.

All of them, at one time or another, have rolled in horse manure.

They like it, it smells good to them, and it's a natural thing for them to do. I explained to them that I hate it when they roll in manure because, to me, it stinks. I told them they would have to stay outside because the manure would get on the walls, the floor, and the furniture. Finally (and I think this was the clincher for Kiska) I told them in no uncertain terms that I *would* bathe them.

Kiska and Duke listened to me and never rolled in manure again. But Dinah cannot stay away from the stinky stuff. It's her natural instinct to roll in it, and she finds it difficult to override that natural inclination, whereas Kiska and Duke were able to do so. In general, I see Dinah's behavior as more wolflike than the other two dogs, and so those natural instincts are more fully ingrained in her. Consequently, our arrangement stands: Whenever she rolls in manure, I bathe her.

Why would an animal disregard your request even after you have stated it in a positive manner and fully explained your reasons?

Sometimes you may think an animal is not listening to what you are saying, but in truth they have their own ideas, or what you might call a predominant purpose, and that's why they are disregarding your requests.

Zachary, a Maine coon cat, would leave his house and property once a week. He would walk down the block, cross a busy street, and end up over a wall in the backyard of a particular house. Even though his people, Alma and Gordon, had explained to him to stay within their own backyard, Zachary would still leave. They had worried about him when he was missing, but when they found out that he was crossing that street with all the cars zooming up and down, they were *really* scared. So they called me for a consultation.

When asked, Zachary explained that the reason he was going to this particular house was because he was teaching something to the cats that lived there. As soon as I related this to his people, Alma exclaimed, "That's just what it looked like when I would go over to get him! He would be sitting facing five cats, and I swear, they looked like they were in school." Zachary assured us that he knew how to cross streets safely and, besides, he was almost finished with those cats and would soon stop leaving his yard.

A month later, Alma and Gordon sent me a note that Zachary had stopped going to his "teaching job" just as he had promised.

They figured school must be out.

Sometimes you can make a deal with your animal to help change a specific behavior problem.

Maybe you have a dog that continually digs up your flower garden. You can say, "Chester, if you will leave my flowers alone, I will take you swimming twice a week." (It also would help if you could give him an alternative by showing him an acceptable place to dig in the yard.)

Or perhaps you have a horse that is constantly trying to return to the barn whenever you're out for a ride. You could say, "Blade, if you would just enjoy our ride together out on the trail for a few hours, I'll give you a piece of sugar when we get back to the barn."

Believe it or not, I have had this method work with ants as well. When I came home to find a huge number of ants in my kitchen, I simply said, "Please, go back from where you came or I will vacuum you." I gave them fifteen minutes and they were gone.

Notice, each time you make a deal with an animal, you ask in the positive way for them *to do* something, instead of the negative way of telling them *not to do* something.

Keep new behavior changes going with positive reinforcement.

Once you have gotten Chester to stop digging up your flowers, be sure to reinforce this wonderful new behavior. When you see him lying peacefully in the yard, say this to him: "Chester, thank you so much for leaving my flowers alone! I like that! You are being very good!"

Or to Blade, you could say, "I had such a good time with you out on the trail today. Thank you for making our ride together such fun."

To the ants, I simply said, "Thank you for going outside."

Something to this effect will help tremendously in keeping Chester, and Blade, and even the ants, on the right track.

Exercise 5

Practice Positive Reinforcement

It's always easier to correct your animals when they are doing something wrong because usually it's an active occurrence of something you don't like. It's hard to remember to acknowledge your animal when they are doing something the right way because it's usually passive, such as Chester lying peacefully in the yard.

- So, look around and notice when your wonderful pet has listened to you about something he or she was doing wrong in the past, but has now changed. This is especially important in the beginning right after an old, unwanted pattern has changed in order to keep the new, acceptable behavior going.

- This could be a cat that was once peeing on the floor and is now using the litter box. You could say, "Thank you, Biscuit, for using the litter box. That really helps me a lot!" Or to a horse who had been chewing on his stall door, but has now stopped, you could say, "Star, I'm so happy you are leaving your stall door alone and only chewing what I give you to eat. Thanks!"

- Practice congratulating your animal companions for the changes they have made in a positive way.

A few words about the human rules . . .

Animals *are* intelligent, but they don't always know, or care, about the human rules. So it's important to let your animal know about the way we humans think things should be.

For instance, one day I asked my own animals to please wipe their feet before coming into the house. One of them looked at me and said, "What's the problem? You don't like the Earth in the house?" They figured that we all live on this planet, Earth, so what was the difference if it was outside or inside? It was all the same to them.

In order to get them to be more careful about their dirty feet, I told my dogs, "People like to have clean floors because, to us, dirt is not always clean, it's hard for us to walk on with our bare feet, and it takes a lot of time for us to clean it up. So, if you guys could just wipe your feet, I would appreciate it. Thank you."

Also remember you must think like a bird, a cat, a snake, and so forth in order to realize what is natural to them. You may have to go back to the first exercise to trigger this thinking.

Many situations occur on a daily basis that might require an explanation about the human rules from a person to an animal friend.

Buster's person, Valerie, wanted to take him on a plane to Dallas with her. She was practicing with Buster by trying to get him to go into an airline dog crate, but he just wouldn't go in, so she called me.

"Does Buster want to go to Dallas with me?" she asked doubtfully. But Buster was excited! He told me that he really wanted to go, but he couldn't understand what sitting in the crate on the back porch had to do with going to Dallas. When I heard what the dog thought, I knew that Buster simply did not understand the human rules.

So I said, "Oh, Valerie, you need to explain to Buster, step-by-step, about car and airplane travel, and why the crate is necessary."

Valerie did a beautiful job of clarifying the matter for the dog. First, she told Buster that they were going to get into the car and put the crate in the backseat. Then, they were going to drive to the airport. When they got to the airport, she was going to ask Buster to get into the crate.

She further explained, "You will have to ride on the plane in this crate, Buster, because it is a human rule." Next she told the dog that he would ride in a compartment in the bottom of the plane while she rode in the top part. Finally, Valerie told Buster that when they got to the airport in Dallas, she would let him out of the crate, and they would spend two glorious weeks together.

As soon as she finished explaining, Valerie told me that Buster looked at her, he looked at the crate, and he went right in.

When Leaving the House: The Basic Four

Your animal has come into your life to be your companion, but when you're not together, what is he or she supposed to be doing? Pets need a purpose or a job while you're gone. And if you thank them for doing what you have asked, they appreciate it. In other words, treat your pet as you would any person who is living with you.

You wouldn't just walk out and not tell your husband, or wife, or roommate that you were leaving, would you? You'd probably tell them where you were going and when you might be back.

Do the same for your animal. As you leave home, tell your pet the basic four:

1. Where you are going
2. When you will return
3. What his or her job is to be
4. Thank you!

This also works well when you have to leave your animal in the car, at a friend's house, or alone under any other circumstance that arises.

When I run to do an errand, I tell my dog Kiska where I'm going. Then I ask him to please take care of the cats and guard the house. I tell him what time I will be returning, and I thank him. I do the same for my cats, although each one may have a different purpose, and none has the same purpose as Kiska.

After clearly stating their purposes several times on separate occasions before leaving, I now just ask them to do their jobs and then say thank you. Or I might say, "Okay, guys, I'm going to town. You know what to do. I'll be back at four-thirty. Thank you."

Can't think of what to tell your companions about their purpose? Here are several suggestions, and after a couple of tries, you'll find your own:

- Look after one another (if you have more than one animal).
- Get well (if they are ill) or stay healthy (if they are fine).
- Keep the house in order.
- Stay in your tank (I've known many fish who have jumped out).
- Have fun.
- Rest.
- Guard the house.
- Be careful.
- You're in charge, make sure everything is fine while I'm gone.

There are other good reasons for speaking to your pet before leaving home besides the fact that it makes them feel comfortable and that your house will still be intact when you return.

I've had clients whose dogs would bark all day after they had left for work. Their neighbors would complain, and by the time I received the call, my clients were at their wit's end. Some were thinking of using bark collars to suppress the barking with a shock, and some were even thinking of having their dog's vocal cords surgically altered.

When I spoke to the dogs about why they were barking, they would say such things to their people as, "Well, where are you going when you leave the house?" and "When are you coming home?" or "Well, what am I supposed to do while you're gone?" or "You didn't tell me what to do so I decided to take care of it myself.

I'm announcing to the neighborhood, 'I'm in charge now. Don't come over here.' "

After my clients began telling their dogs the Basic Four, all was quiet on the home front.

You can see how some thoughtful communication before leaving home helped to resolve these particular situations. Now that you know this, be sure to incorporate the Basic Four as one of your daily interactions with your animal friends.

My clients who have horses tell them something similar when they leave the barn to go home. They explain that they are leaving and that they will see them tomorrow, next Tuesday, or whenever they think they will return. Then they thank their horses for cooperating with whomever is taking care of them. Several of my clients have told their horses to get well, if they happened to be injured, as part of their job. (Of course, you can do this, as mentioned earlier, with whatever animal you have if they are not well when you leave them at home, the kennel, or the veterinarian's office.)

My client Nancy told me that Kokomo, her bay gelding, had injured his fetlock. She would visit him every day, and every day as she left she would say, "I'll see you tomorrow, Kokomo. Your job is to get well so we can go riding again soon. Thank you. I love you."

Telling your pet where you are going is especially important before you leave on vacation.

It's important because it seems many animals pick this time to leave home. If you tell them all the facts, your pet is more likely to wait at home for you, and not worry about where you are or when you will return.

Be sure to tell Sasha where you are going, what day you're planning to return, that Aunt Sally is going to take care of her, and to please stay in the yard for Aunt Sally while you are away.

I further encourage my clients to make this statement to their animals: "*I'm* going on vacation, so now, I want *you* to be on vacation, too. Please take a break from all the work you do for me. Relax and have a good time with Aunt Sally."

Or if your animals are going to a kennel, tell them the previously mentioned information about going on vacation, and then further instruct them to have fun with the other dogs or cats, along with any other pertinent information. You get the idea.

Send positive thoughts while you're away on vacation.

While you're on vacation and have left your animal in the best possible care, send them only positive thoughts when thinking of them.

Your pet can pick up on your thoughts even when you're miles away, and if you worry, he or she may needlessly start to worry as well. Here's a perfect example.

Patty went on a trip leaving her two dogs with a capable pet sitter, but the whole time she was away, she worried that her dogs wouldn't eat while she was gone. As soon as Patty came home, the sitter told her that everything was fine, except her dogs had barely taken a bite of food.

When the dogs were asked why they hadn't touched their food while Patty was away, they replied, "Well, we knew you were worried about us eating, so we thought something was wrong with the food and decided not to eat it." (Remember, they pick up on the pictures in our minds, not the intention!)

You see why it's a good idea to send joyful thoughts to your animal while you're on a trip, or for that matter, any time.

Remember, animals live in the moment.

Though they understand linear time because they live with us, their natural state is being in the present moment.

One of the many gifts that an animal gives you is showing you how to be in the moment. They are right here, right now.

When you are in the moment, you are neither anxious about something that has yet to happen in the future, nor upset or guilty over something that happened in the past.

It's not that a dog doesn't remember that he pooped on the floor an hour ago, it's just he has moved on—he's in the here and now, the present moment.

Be very specific when asking an animal about a certain situation.

When Patricia asked Holly, her golden retriever, who was lying down, how she was feeling, Holly said she was fine.

"But," her person protested, "what about that limp you have?"

"Ohhh, the limp," Holly replied. "Well that's just something that happened yesterday when I stepped down too hard on a rock."

Because she was comfortable lying down, the pain in Holly's foot didn't concern her at *that* moment.

*Use precise questions
to get the information
you are seeking from
your pet.*

Many times in my consultations, a person calls me because his or her animal is having a health issue or a behavioral problem, but instead of asking the animal specifically about that problem, the client asks something general like, "Baron, what's going on?" Baron then proceeds to tell me something unrelated to the problem at hand and does not address the real issue his person wishes to know about—just as Holly did in the prior example.

Get specific, get to the point, and as I tell my clients, be a detective. Dig around and ask as much as you can about the particular issue you want to know about.

Be specific. Ask Baron why he snapped at that child yesterday when she came into the house. This will help you to receive a very specific answer, which will then assist you to more easily resolve the issue. So that the next time you can avoid a scary or dangerous situation, such as Baron frightening a child.

So even if you can't yet hear your animal friend, you can speak to them.

And in just speaking to them, you will be amazed at some of the results you will get. Remember, that the more intelligently you treat your pet, the more intelligent the action you will see coming back at you will be.

Now that you've explored some of the basics about learning to talk to animals, it's time to examine ways to listen to them.

But first . . . let's recap Part One.

Part I Recap
Speaking to Your Animals

1. Imagine what it feels like to be an animal.
2. Recognize your pet's intelligence.
3. Get your animal's attention.
4. Speak to your pet as you would a person.
5. Say exactly what you mean.
6. State a request in the positive.
7. Be precise in what you ask.
8. Explain the reasons behind your requests.
9. Make a deal with your animal, if necessary, to change a specific behavior.
10. Use positive reinforcement after your animal has changed an unacceptable behavior.
11. As you leave home, inform your pet where you are going, when you will return, and what her or his purpose is while you are away.
12. Remember your love for your animal companion and thank him or her for listening.

PART II

Getting the Message

Hearing Your Animal

How do you hear animals?

How do you go about the process of re-membering this ability we were all born with that lies buried in us like some treasure buried beneath the ocean? What can you do to dredge up this skill that is, indeed, a treasure?

This is the question that people ask most. And it's the part that most everyone struggles with—getting *what* their animal is trying to tell them.

All it takes for some people is to just discover that they *can* perceive messages from their animals, they get it and can do it right away. Others, such as several of my clients, will open to this gift after one or two consultations with an animal communicator. And some people, such as myself, must do extensive work on themselves before they can hear the animals.

What you are trying to
hear is very subtle.

What you are trying to experience is subtle. Even after you practice and work at communicating with an animal, the feeling of what you are receiving can be quite elusive. It's rarely going to be as blatant as the words you hear out of a person's mouth. So realize the subtlety of what you are about to perceive.

Where do I begin?

First, sit quietly with your animal and have a sincere desire to hear.

With so much commotion in our daily lives, both inside our heads and in our environment, we need to be quiet. After all, if the television is on, and the phone is ringing, or you can't stop thinking about what your mother said to you this morning, how can you perceive a subtle thought from your animal?

Previous experience with meditation may help you, but it isn't necessary. What *is* necessary is a *sincere desire*. You have to *want* to communicate with an animal before you can actually hear anything from him or her. So you must have a sincere desire to perceive, to hear, to feel, to intuit what your animal is trying to communicate to you.

Exercise 6

Being Quiet with Your Animal

- Get quiet. Still your mind. Just be with your cat or your bird, or your horse, or your dog, or whatever delightful creature has come to live with you. It might actually be a relief to take time out from the stressful business that our lives have become.

- Get in touch with the love you have for your wonderful companion.

- Observe the way your animal's body looks. Stare at one part of his or her body, like the tip of an ear, and let your focus go soft. What do you see? Does it fade out to white? Or maybe you see your animal's body appear to wave in a pattern. Perhaps you see the body appear to become made up of little dots. Possibly you simply notice a detail that's evaded you before.

Whatever you see or feel will help you to shift your focus for this new experience of perceiving information from your animal companion.

- And don't forget that sincere desire.

Abby sat with her kitten Biscuit on her chest. In the quiet, she noticed that they both were breathing at the same rate. Then—looking eye to eye—she began to fully notice Biscuit's remarkable asymmetrical coloring. How it made the most amazing abstract "painting" of color and design across her beloved animal's face. Those few calm, *shared* moments helped Abby to center and to open to the subtle messages from Biscuit in their conversation.

Exercise 7

Pretend to Be
an Animal Trying
to Communicate
with a Person

This exercise is not unlike Exercise 1 where you chose an animal and slipped into his or her body. This time, select any animal you wish, and feel what it's like to try to communicate with a person.

- First, as in exercise one, pick an animal, move into that body, and experience some of the feelings that that animal may have—walking, climbing a tree, flying, being on the lookout for predators, galloping along a trail, and so forth.

Now, here are some examples of the type of questions you could ask yourself, depending on the animal you choose.

- What does it feel like to be a horse trying to let a person know that your saddle is cinched too tightly?

- What does it feel like to be a cat trying to let your person know that you really need the litter box upstairs in the bathroom, not downstairs in the basement?

- What does it feel like to be a ferret trying to tell a person that you would so much like to have another ferret come to live with you?

- What does it feel like to be a dog trying to tell a person that the flea collar you are wearing is making you dizzy and giving you a headache?

- Continue thinking of other things you'd like to tell your person as the animal you picked to be.

- Play around with this exercise and move into the body of several different species and, again, experience the need to communicate with your person.

Next, intend to hear.

Say to yourself, "I intend to hear my cat Chloe." This helps to set you up to succeed. Continue by saying, "I intend to hear her in the most honest and loving and objective manner possible." And part of what that means is to rid yourself of your own human ideas and feelings.

A client of mine, Jason, called me because he couldn't find his cat, Chelsea. It was freezing outside, and he was worried that Chelsea might get sick or, even worse, freeze to death. When I spoke to the cat, she reported that she was just fine and, to her, it wasn't cold; she had plenty of fur.

This is a simple example, but you get the idea. Leave your human conceptions on the back burner.

Try to leave your own emotions out of what you hear.

Remember that animals have their own individual feelings and ideas about things, some of which may seem odd, or foreign, or even impossible to you.

Don't let the fact that you may hear something strange deter you from thinking it could be true. In fact, if this is the case, so much the better because this probably would be something that would never occur to you except that you *did hear it* from another species and not in your own mind.

One of my first consultations involved a woman, her two cats, and an Irish setter named Maggie. Among other questions the woman asked of her companions was what was their purpose with her. When it was the setter's turn to answer, I heard her say, "My purpose is to love you, to hold you, and comfort you." When I heard that, I thought to myself that this sounded like a marriage vow, and how did a dog hold a person, anyway? I considered not telling the woman what I had heard, but my job is to tell the client in the most honest and loving manner possible everything that I hear, regardless of whether it makes sense to me or not. As soon as I told her, the woman exclaimed, "I can't believe she told you that! Every night when I come home from work, Maggie greets me by sitting up on her haunches, placing all four legs around me, and just holding me. I've always felt she was telling me she loved me, and she was there to comfort me after a hard day."

It was a good reminder to keep my reactions out of what I'd heard, and the same goes for you when listening to your companion.

*Start by speaking to
your animal
companion.*

Generally, you will want to first speak to your animal before you hear from him or her.

You may want to ask a question, or you may simply want to tell your companion something you feel is important, and then see how your animal responds. Either way, be sure to remember what you learned in Part One about speaking to your pet: Be sure that what you say is not only stated clearly and positively, but also matches what you see in your mind.

Move your focus out of your head.

It seems as though most of us live in our heads. You feel that your brain is whirring away up there, and you see from your eyes up there, and you hear up there, and taste, and eat, and talk . . . But you're *not* going to hear your animal in your head. You're going to hear your animal in your heart.

As Kevin Ryerson says in his book *Spirit Communication: The Soul's Path,* "God is in the human heart and is the vehicle by which we can communicate directly with one another."

Exercise 8

Moving Your Focus Down into Your Heart

- Sit quietly and take a few deep, full breaths. You may want to close your eyes.

- Place your hand on your throat.

- Then swallow and focus on your throat.

- Now move your hand and focus lower and lower, until your hand is on your heart.

- Feel your heart beating.

- Next, go into that place in your heart I call the tender spot, that place that almost hurts. That place that feels so tender when you think of how much you love your pets; the ones that are living and even the ones that are no longer with you. Sometimes those animals that are gone are the ones that help us most to feel that tender spot.

As the writer Coelho so eloquently put it, "Where your treasure is, there also will be your heart . . . Be aware of the place where you are brought to tears. That's where your heart is and where your treasure is."

After you are able to find this tender spot a few times, you won't have to go through this exercise, you'll just immediately go to that place in your heart.

Letting the communication come into your heart.

So, you have asked your question and you have moved into your heart. You are in that tender spot, and now let the words, or feelings, or colors, or the pictures come into your heart.

Think of a Valentine, a symbol for the heart. It is the image of two ears put together. Two ears join to form a heart. This is an idea to keep in mind as you practice.

Or perhaps you could keep this image in mind: **HEAR = HEAR**T.

Let the messages come in—don't try so hard to hear, don't strain to hear, just let them come gently in. Sit back, relax, and let them flow into your open heart.

This is a feeling of unforced expectation.

These words, or pictures, or colors, or feelings—and remember, all are valid—will come to you in an instant.

They come quickly at what I call the speed of thought.

Pay attention and catch them.

If you think you heard something, or saw something, or felt something, then *believe* that you did.

One of my clients, Bethann, was trying to communicate with her close companion, Dubie, who is a darling Maltese. She called me because she was having a bit of trouble, so I explained to her about listening with her heart. Bethann hung up and went to give it a try. She called me back a short time later to tell me that after we spoke, she had been lying on the bed with Dubie, and then she had placed one hand on her own heart and one hand on Dubie's heart, just to make sure the conversation was heart to heart. After describing the scene, she asked me, "Do the words and pictures come really fast? Do they come so fast that you just think something came whizzing by, but you're not sure and you almost miss it?" I answered excitedly, "That's it, Bethann. You've got it!"

And with great satisfaction, she calmly replied, "If that's the case, then I heard her."

Accept whatever you perceive.

If you discount what you perceive, you may be rejecting your animal's efforts to communicate with you, and after a while they may stop trying.

But more likely they will continue with you as long as you are sincerely making an attempt.

As Brave Buffalo of Standing Rock Indian Reservation said: "The animals want to communicate with man. But Wakan-Tanka [God] does not intend that they should do so directly. Man must do the greater part in securing an understanding."

Exercise 9

Validating What You Hear

The moment you think you've got something, *anything,* write it down. Then read it aloud and ask yourself these questions:

- *Did I know that piece of information before?* You may have known, or you may say to yourself, "Gee, I didn't know that."

- *Do the words sound like something I would say?* Or do they sound different from your own? Perhaps they sound more formal, more eloquent, more serious, or maybe funnier than yours.

- *Does the feeling I just got feel like something I have ever felt before?* Or is this a new way of feeling about something you have just asked your animal. Perhaps you can feel the way moist dirt feels on the pads of your dog's or cat's feet. Maybe you can feel the fear a horse feels at seeing a shadow across a trail.

- *If you got a picture, try to write down all the details you saw.* Look back inside your mind at that picture. Look all around it and pick out every tiny detail, and put them all down on paper.

The purpose of this exercise is to help you distinguish between your own thoughts and those of your animal companion.

Some people get words, others get feelings or colors, and still others get pictures.

You may just get a feeling, but not words. And that's okay. I happen to get words and pictures, but no feelings. I can usually tell an animal's attitude by the way he or she says something, so I do sort of know how an animal feels about what is being said.

One of my clients, who recently opened to this ability, gets only colors and is somehow able to interpret them in understanding his six dogs. It's a mystery to me.

A couple of house sitters I know can walk into your house and know many things about your pets right away. The first time I watched them do this, I was amazed, and when I told them how incredibly wonderful I thought they were, they both said, "But, Judy, I can't hear the way *you can*." I replied, "You don't need to, you just *know*."

So add this bit of information to your growing arsenal of knowledge. You may just "know" what an animal wants or is trying to tell you. And that's something very special.

A few tips that may help you.

- When you first begin, it's easier to have someone else ask a question of the animal you are trying to communicate with so you can more easily stay focused in your heart. When you have to formulate a question, generally, you are using your mind and, consequently, are more focused in your head.

- Close your eyes so that the animal's cute, physical body doesn't distract you from thinking that there is intelligence in there.

- You may want to try a "practice" session with someone else's pet. Have a friend that you're comfortable with ask his or her animal companion a question. You just listen, and then you tell your friend what you perceived. If your friend already knew this bit of information about his or her pet, but you did not, then hooray! I call this getting confirmation that you are, indeed, hearing an animal's message.

You may be able to hear your animal companion right away because you have never lost the ability to do so, and just reading this book will trigger your memory or intuition.

As I mentioned in the preface, you were born with the ability to intuitively communicate. I'm sure you, at one time or another, have experienced that feeling of knowing something beforehand, such as when you pick up the phone and know exactly who is on the other end of the line. That is intuition. And this is the ability you use to receive messages from your animal companion.

What happened to cause you to lose this precious gift? Actually, you never lost it; you just suppressed it because of the nature of our society. When you were a baby, everyone was coaxing you to talk—"Say, 'Mommy'; say, 'Dada.' " No one was talking about communicating silently through intuition, even though many parents intuitively know what a baby wants.

It is possible to remember how to use this gift, and that's why I say that just reading this book may trigger your memory.

You may have already heard your pet many times and just not realized it.

I have a client, Alexis, who called me because she wanted to know if her new dog, Destiny, would like to go with her to cheer up people by visiting them in a nearby retirement home. I had Alexis explain to the dog every detail about what was involved in visiting frail and sometimes sick, older people. Then Alexis asked Destiny if she would like to do this. The dog answered that she would and added that this was the reason she had come to Alexis. Alexis found that remarkable because the same thought had crossed her mind the day she found Destiny as a stray running down the road near her house.

This had been a month or so after Alexis's dog Contessa had died, and Contessa had often gone with her to the retirement home. Alexis had thought that maybe this new dog would take up the work that Contessa had done at the home, and that's why she had named her Destiny. Alexis missed doing this work with Contessa, so now hearing that Destiny had come to continue that work made Alexis happy.

Like Alexis, you may already have had ideas or thoughts or feelings from your pet, but had no reason to think they were not your own.

When Alexis first picked up the stray dog she named Destiny, she thought the dog would like to do the work with her at the retirement home.

Why would she think this? She had actually heard it from Destiny, but just assumed it was her own thoughts flashing by.

Several clients have contacted me to do a consultation with their pets, and after one or two consults, they call me back and say . . .

"Judy, I can hear them!" When I learn this, it makes me feel like I've just scored the winning basket in the championship game of the NCAA tournament. And I say *Yessssss!* because I just scored one for the home team—our animal companions. This gives me the greatest joy because that's what I'm going for. I want everyone to be able to hear his or her own animal companions, as well as wild animals.

Frankie called me because her yellow Labrador, Honey, was eating poop from her cat's litter box. After hearing Honey's reasons for doing this, I had Frankie explain to her why this was unacceptable. Additionally, I suggested some changes in the Lab's diet that might also help the situation. Frankie called me two weeks later to report that Honey had stopped eating the cat poop, but more exciting to Frankie was the revelation that she was now able to hear Honey.

Frankie told me that she and Honey had gone for a walk in the national forest. Honey had run too far ahead of Frankie as she had done many times before, and this always made Frankie very nervous. She was terribly afraid that Honey wouldn't come back or that the dog might get lost. But this time things were different. When Frankie called Honey, she clearly heard her dog say, "Don't worry. I'm busy checking out a rabbit hole." As Frankie rounded the next bend in the path, she came upon Honey with her nose in what looked like a rabbit hole. She was relieved, but more, she was thrilled that she had heard her dog!

All it took was doing just one consultation and Frankie remembered her innate ability to intuitively communicate with her animal companion.

Be patient with yourself. If you don't hear right away, keep trying.

You may be able to perceive sometimes, and then other times you will hear nothing. Sometimes you may receive only a fragment of an idea. Be sure to ask for more information. You may have to read a few more books on the subject, or go to an animal-communication workshop. Different animal-communication specialists listed in the appendix hold these all over the country. Remember, this is a process that takes time. You didn't learn to walk overnight, either. It took me two years and a lot of work before I was able to hear the animals consistently. You may have to do some work on yourself, as I did, in order to remove any blocks or problems that you may have that are keeping you from hearing your animal.

My problem was that I had locked down my heart. Yours may be different. Your obstacle could be due to a fear that you are not good enough or worthy enough to be able to intuit what an animal is sending you. You *are* good enough.

It could be that other people, perhaps your family members or friends, make comments that animal communication isn't possible, undermining your belief in it, and consequently, those comments weaken your efforts. Trust your own instincts and your heart.

*You may block what
you hear because
intuitive
communication is so
subtle that you can't
believe it's real.*

It *is* real. Or you may think that you have to go to school and get some sort of degree or certificate to validate this work as real. But remember that you were born with this ability to intuitively get messages from animals, so no school can claim that you need a degree to practice this natural gift.

You've already got your degree.

I previously mentioned that you might need to read a few more books on animal communication, or perhaps you might need to take an animal-communication workshop, but the following story shows you don't need to overdo it.

Adrienne used to make an appointment with me every week to do a consultation with her magnificent wolf hybrid, Cheyenne. She mainly called to see if she was indeed hearing what Cheyenne had communicated to her at some point during the week. Adrienne always was right on the money in getting what Cheyenne had been communicating, but the woman was never confident that she was really getting the pictures her wolf was sending. She had taken several animal-communication workshops and many meditation seminars over a five-year period and, yet, she still felt the need to take even more classes of some sort or another before she could really hear Cheyenne.

I could tell that Cheyenne was actually becoming exasperated with Adrienne, so finally I said to her, "Adrienne! Trust yourself and stop 'studenting' yourself to death!" I guess I said it so forcefully that Adrienne was somewhat taken aback. Then she laughed and said I was right.

Now I only hear from Adrienne every few months just to keep me abreast of her wonderful progress. She has stopped taking every class that comes along, and she and Cheyenne are doing great.

So do the work that it takes to reconnect with this gift.

It's worth it not only so you can hear your pet but also because it will be of great benefit to you personally. As I discovered in the work I did on myself, opening to hearing my animal companions also opened my heart to many other important aspects of myself and the world around me.

Now once you get going and start to get your animal companion's messages, remember to acknowledge what you have just heard.

For instance, if your animal tells you, "I love you," what would you say in return? You could say, "I love you, too," or you could say, "Thank you, I know you do," or whatever feels appropriate.

Maybe your companion agrees to some new behavior that you've just suggested. Do you simply rush on to the next question? No. It would be suitable to say, "Thank you," or "I'm so glad you agreed to this new rule," or "I appreciate that. It certainly will make my life easier. "But *don't* just go on to the next question.

In your initial amazement that you're actually perceiving messages, you can forget to acknowledge your animal companion.

Remember, you're having a conversation.

If an animal says something you don't understand, question them until you are satisfied with what they are trying to tell you. If your pet says something that you disagree with, say so. You are having a give-and-take conversation with an intelligent being. That's part of the joy.

Keep an open heart and an open mind and you will be amazed at what you can achieve by communicating openly with your animal companion.

Part II Recap
Getting the Message

1. Sit quietly with your animal and have a sincere desire to hear.
2. Pretend to be an animal trying to communicate with a person.
3. Set your intention to hear.
4. Leave your own emotions and sympathetic reactions out of what you hear.
5. Start by speaking to the animal.
6. Move your focus out of your head and into your heart.
7. Respect whatever words, pictures, colors, or feelings you perceive.
8. Validate what you hear, no matter how subtle.
9. In the beginning, have someone else ask a question of the animal while you just listen.
10. At first, keep your eyes closed so the animal's physical body does not distract you.
11. Keep trying if you don't hear right away.
12. Acknowledge what you hear from the animal before moving on to the next question.
13. Remember, you're having a give-and-take conversation.
14. Keep an open mind and an open heart

Frequently Asked Questions

Are all species intelligent?

Yes.

Does this animal-communication stuff work with all kinds of animals?

Yes, most definitely. In this book I mainly write about cats, dogs, and horses, but it works with any animal with which you wish to communicate. This would include birds, reptiles, insects, spiders, fish, and, of course, mammals.

Will my animal still listen even if I can't hear him?

Yes.

Will I be able to get behavioral changes in my animal even if I can't hear her?

Yes.

Why would I want to talk with my pet?

There are so many reasons, but the most significant ones are:

- To understand your pet's behavior.
- To gain harmony in your relationship
- To avoid drastic measures resulting from unacceptable animal behavior, such as giving away a child's beloved rabbit because she pees on the carpet, or taking a dog to the shelter because he continues to escape from the backyard, or euthanizing a cat because he's killing birds in the yard.

What is intuition?

It's something we all have. It's the ability to know or sense something without the use of traditional processes. It is immediate cognition or what you might call perceptive insight.

Do animals have a memory?

Yes. However, remember they move beyond the past and live in the present. A good lesson for all of us.

Appendix

A source of animal communicators as well as a source for all levels of animal communication workshops around the country and abroad:

Species Link: A Journal of Interspecies Communication
Published quarterly by Pegasus Publications
P.O. Box 1060, Point Reyes, CA 94956
(415) 663-1247

An animal communicator that I would recommend who is not listed in *Species Link*:

Deb Jones
Venice Beach, California
(310) 305-1552

Books of similar interest:

Kinship with All Life by J. Allen Boone (Harper San Francisco, 1954).
Beyond Obedience by April Frost (New York: Harmony Books, 1998).
Talking with Nature by Michael Roads (Tiburon, CA: H. J. Kramer, 1988).
Animal Talk by Penelope Smith (Point Reyes Station, CA: Pegasus, 1982; 1989).

A source of animal communicators is also listed in the back of:

Communicating with Animals: The Spiritual Connection Between People and Animals by Arthur Myers (Chicago: Contemporary Books, 1997).

About the Author

JUDY MEYER has been changing the lives of pets and their people as an intuitive animal communicator since 1990. With more than 800 clients throughout the United States, Canada, England, and Germany, Judy works with an open heart and generosity of spirit that enable animals and their humans to understand and overcome physical and psychological difficulties.

She lives in a sanctuary-like setting in Tesuque, New Mexico, with her seven cats, two dogs, and the birds, lizards, snakes, ants, spiders, skunks, raccoons, rabbits, coyotes, and bears who live in the area, and sometimes come around her house.

Judy can be reached for consultation and private one-on-one workshops at (505) 820-PETS [7387].